# Hazy Sunshine

Between the blur & the break, the sun found
a way.

Pratik Madnani

BookLeaf
Publishing

India | USA | UK

Made with ❤ on the BookLeaf Publishing Platform
www.bookleafpub.in
www.bookleafpub.com

# Dedication

**To you, the reader,**
who picked up this book searching for light,
may you find pieces of yourself in these pages -
the soft, the brave, the still-growing.

**And to my wife,**
the quiet constant,
whose love lit every corner I once thought too dark.
*This book carries your strength between its lines.*

# Preface

*This book was never meant to be loud.*

It was never meant to shout over pain or decorate it with glitter. It was written in the hush that follows a storm - in the space where things break, and then begin to heal.

_Hazy Sunshine_ is a collection born from the grey. From in-between seasons. From mornings that weren't quite bright, but still promised warmth. These pages carry fragments of survival, softness, silence, and strength - the kind that doesn't always roar, but stays anyway.

Some pieces were written in the middle of it all. Some came after. Some I didn't know were still inside me. But each one is something I chose to keep.
If you've ever stood in the blur between who you were and who you're becoming - this is for you.

Here's to the almost-light,
to the moments that didn't shine,
but stayed anyway.

# Acknowledgements

This book is not a celebration of perfection.
It is a tribute to survival.
To the days that broke me - thank you.
You taught me how to rebuild.
To the nights I couldn't breathe,
and still chose to stay - this book carries your strength.

Every piece in *Hazy Sunshine* was born from the ache of
trying to hold on,
and the quiet courage it took not to give up.
To every version of myself that refused to be defined by
the storm;
You didn't shatter,
You softened.

And that softness became light.
Thank you to the pain, the pause, the pull of giving up;
For each gave me the choice to bloom instead.
And I did.
-Pratik Madnani

# When No One's Watching

In a world where light glows on blue screens,
and clicks or reactions are currencies
I ask, how much are you willing to do, when nobody's
watching?
When there is no one to measure the angle of your smile,
or double tap to give a heart.

Who are you ?
And who do you choose to be ?

This is an era of mirrors and masks,
filters and fading flashes,
where we race to be seen, liked, known.
But, somewhere in the corner, when you sit alone
You realise, it is not the gleams of filters or frames
What matters is
the patience you pour into places that don't shine back.

# The Toe Fracture

I remember,
a few years back,
I had a toe fracture -
on one of my birthdays.
I felt really bad that on a good day,
something so painful happened to me.
The next day, I went to an orthopaedic surgeon,
and he wrapped my toe
with the adjacent one, using a tape.
And surprisingly,
it didn't hurt that much.

Maybe that's why
we need a hug,
we need to be wrapped,
on our broken days,

just to ease the pain.

# Sometimes, Just Accept

The thing is -
We've always been taught to *chase*.
Chase grades.
Chase jobs.
Chase whatever comes next.
We're trained to run,
but never taught
how to *pause*,
how to *acknowledge*.

Sometimes,
you don't need to rush.
The thing with pain is -
it's not meant to be buried.
You have to *understand* it,
not just cover it up.
Because wounds may heal,
but they leave behind scars.
And sometimes,
you simply have to accept

that you carry those scars.
There's no shame in that.

Acknowledgment.
Acceptance.

They won't erase the pain -
but they'll let you breathe.
They'll let you stop running.
Even if just for a moment.

# This is not the End

I know—

Times are tough.

Anxiety is real.

So here are **50 reasons not to end your life**:

1. Your parents. Your family. Your friends - they'll miss you deeply.
2. Life is still worth living.
3. The clouds
4. Sunrises and sunsets, painting the sky just for you.
5. Hills and oceans.
6. Birthdays of friends and their friends.
7. You are worthy - of love, patience, and everything in between.
8. Pizza and pasta. Simple joys.
9. Movies that make you laugh, cry, feel.
10. I don't even know you, but I love you. Truly.
11. Your smile - please, let it stay.

12. Your dreams. They matter.
13. Rain tapping on your window.
14. Bad days do disappear.
15. Music that speaks when words fail.
16. Butterflies and flowers - gentle reminders of life's softness.
17. Who else will laugh at the silly things you and your friends do?
18. Deep down, you do have a reason to live.
19. Kisses.
20. Dogs. Always dogs.
21. Drunk nights and the stories that follow.
22. Theme parks. The thrill. The cotton candy.
23. Life isn't punishing you - it's testing your strength.
24. Your celebrity crush still hasn't met you.
25. That feeling of wearing new clothes.
26. Sneakers.
27. Your teachers are still proud of you.
28. Waterfalls. Magic in motion.
29. Loud music - and annoying your neighbours.
30. Coffee that warms your hands and soul.
31. You are beautiful.
32. Someone would die for you. (Not literally, but still.)
33. Saturday nights and spontaneous plans.
34. There's always a reason to begin again.

35. Stars. The moon. The sky watching over you.

36. Cupcakes. Cheesecakes.

37. The love your parents gave just to bring you here.

38. Someone cares. They just don't know how to say it.

39. Traveling. The world is waiting to meet you.

40. Books. Pages that understand you.

41. Let your bullies envy your survival and your smile.

42. Adventures you haven't taken yet.

43. Strangers who could become lifelines.

44. Your story - your struggle - is not in vain.

45. Long drives with no destination.

46. You've already changed someone's life - you just don't know it.

47. First dates, awkward laughs, and warm hands.

48. Growing old and annoying people with grace.

49. Bubble wrap. Pop away your stress.

50. You.

**Yes, YOU.**


I could write a thousand more.

Please, talk to someone.

There's no shame in sharing.

Ending your life won't end the pain - it only passes it on.

# New Leaves

The thing about life is -
It's unpredictable.
You can't count on anything.
Winter may linger,
making your heart feel frozen.

But that's the thing about seasons:
Spring always follows.
And with it,

a fresh bloom
of brand new leaves.

# Steps, Not Leaps

They say success is a crown,
glimmering on the heads of the bold.
But very few speak about the grind,
the slow, silent push that makes one pass through the
blur.
There is a point in the journey where the sparkle dims
and the path is dusted with repetition.
The great ones?
They kept going,
when the morning feels like yesterday's shadow and task
seems to be nothing new.
But, the rhythm of small steps creates a dance.

**It's not the leap, but the step.**

Not the breakthrough, but the build up.
So,
keep doing, keep walking
through the flat roads, endless activities of sameness,
As the climb is hidden in those steps you take


Again & Again.

# Sit where Souls speaks

Sit at a table
where the stars feel closer,
and the talk is about dreams, not people.

Speak of the universe,
how it feels endless, yet connected to us all.

Talk about goals -
the ones that scare you and excite you at once.
Share stories of what you want to build,
not what others have done.

Money? Discuss it as a tool,
something to build a better life,
not as the measure of your worth.

And God - talk about the wonders of life,
the little signs that keep you moving forward.

Leave the tables
where people's lives are dissected like puzzles,
where gossip fills the space
but leaves your soul empty.

Sit with those who lift you,
who make you think bigger,
who remind you that your dreams matter.

Because in those moments,
you're growing,
you're alive,
you're reaching for the stars.

# Trophies No One Sees

The world claps loudest
for trophies it can see
titles, numbers,
names on screens.
But your quiet wins?
They live in the silence of healing,
in the courage to try again,
in the smile you wear
after nights that broke you.

They won't make headlines,
but they made YOU.

Maybe success
isn't always loud,
maybe it's the whisper
that says,
"I'm proud of you,"
when no one else knows
what it took to stand.

So let the world cheer its way.
You just keep building
your own kind of brave.

# Light on the other side

You sit in the dark,
walls breathing silence,
the air filled with questions,
that, only you can hear.
There's a window -
always was.

But light doesn't barge in
without permission.
You have to rise,
even if your knees tremble,
even if your hands feel cold.

You have to reach -
pull open the latch
with hope.
Because no one else
can open your window.

No one else
can choose the light
for you.

And the day you do
even a crack,
you'll realize:
the darkness
was never stronger
than your will
to see through it.

# Every Day, a Little More

...and that's how it has always been.
It was never about *leaving* the comfort zone
just stretching it, gently,
a little more each day.

Life doesn't follow a script.
One moment you're full
of joy, of peace
and the next, it all unravels
without warning.
But if there's one thing
these years with myself have taught me,
it's this:
Be humble when you're flying high,
and be grateful
when you're down low
because both are teachers,
both are temporary.

No one truly likes
sad endings in real life.
And if where you are
doesn't feel like the ending you deserve,
don't wait for a savior.
Be your own.
Dream louder.
Work harder.
And build the ending

that once felt too far
to even glance.

# The Tiny Creature

**One fine evening, I was heading back home.**
It was dark.
And somehow, I felt... I hadn't taken the shorter route.
Instead, I had chosen a path that seemed to stretch
endlessly -
one that felt unfamiliar, and far from home.
On the way, I came across a tiny creature.
It looked up at me and asked softly,
*"Where are you heading?"*
I paused.
"I don't really know," I said.
"I think I've taken the wrong path.
I feel... lost."

It tilted its head and asked,
*"Do you want to share anything else?"*

"Yes," I whispered.
"I just feel... like I'm missing something.
Not something specific, but a constant sense

that something's absent.
I'm not even sure what it is.
And maybe I'm so out of my mind,
I took the wrong path and ended up in this place -
this dark, confusing place."

The creature looked at me with calm, knowing eyes,
and then said:
**"Close your eyes... and listen.**
It is always in the darkest hour
that we find our strength.
We blame ourselves too much -
for everything.
But not every day is meant to be the same.
You will walk through dark paths.
And through them, you will find your way.
You don't need to seek shelter for your soul
in someone else.
You need to plant it within *you*.
On the days life feels cruel,
don't mirror that cruelty back to yourself.
Breathe.
Let go of the memories that weigh you down.
Be kind to yourself.
Don't underestimate your worth.
And don't look around for sympathy —
you are not made for pity.

Keep walking,
until your heart tells you it's time to rest.
When a tree grows,
it faces the sun, the storms, the seasons.
And yet, it grows.
*You are a tree.*
Your roots must be strong -
to survive the harshness and
to drink in the light when it comes.
So water yourself.
Let the light cut through your darkness.
The light is within you.
It has always been within you."


To anyone who feels lost -
**You are your tiny creature.**

# Racing Shadows

No point in racing shadows
when your sun rises from a different sky.

They walk through deserts
while you swim through storms.

Both are battles,
both are brave.

Comparison is a thief
that robs you
of the quiet victory
you live each day.

You are swimming, they are climbing.
Your success is depth; theirs is height.

Breathe - you aren't behind.
You are on your own journey;
they are on their own.

# Not Perfect, Still Whole

You won't always get what you crave,
Not everything will fall in place,
But the world isn't empty of chances.

You have hands, you have heart,
You have the power to create,
From the scraps life gives you,
You can build, shape, form.
Blame is a chain that holds you back,
A story where you play the victim
But in that role, you lose the plot.

Take what's in front of you,
Even if it's small, or broken, or bruised,
And make something beautiful from it.

*A puzzle missing pieces can still be a picture,*
*A song without perfect notes can still sing.*

*You're not trapped by what you lack,*
*But liberated by what you choose to do with what you*
*have.*

So rise, because -
In every crack, there's a chance to shine,
And from what's broken, something new is born.

# With Whom It Flows

**And one day,**
You will meet someone
With whom the conversations will never seem to end.
Someone who will ask you -
Where were you born?
Who will want to know all your nicknames,
how you fell off a bicycle and broke your hand,
how many pets you had while growing up,
the love you carry for the blues in the sky,
and the fear that creeps in with the dark at night.

They'll ask about the flavour of ice cream
you cried for as a child,
the dish that felt like home,
how your mother took care of everything,
and how you used to sleep at 8 P.M sharp.
They'll want to hear about
how your grandparents passed away,
how your clothes still rest on that one chair,
and your socks lie near your shoes.

They'll ask about your long-held dreams,
the things you loved so much you let go,
your journey through ups and downs,
your weaknesses, your strengths,
your insecurities and fears.
They'll want to know -
your favourite song, your guilty pleasures, your regrets,
the bond you share with your parents and siblings,
how you stare at things you want but put them back
after seeing the price tag,
what pisses you off,
what breaks you quietly from within.
They'll ask about your past
and how it still walks with you,
about the time nobody stood by your side
when you only needed one hand to hold.
They'll want to know your darkest secrets,
and how you enjoy light-hearted conversations,
how you don't like dancing in pubs when drunk,
how you like to kiss,
how you gaze at stars and listen to the sea,
your trips to the mountains,
your inside and your outside -
every bit of you.

**You will meet someone.**

With whom the conversations will never seem to end.

# Not Lost, Just Hidden

They say, "Discover yourself"
I say, you aren't lost.

Are you are a treasure buried in distant sands,
Waiting for a map to reveal ?

*No, your truth lies not in discovery*
*it rests in uncovering.*

Beneath the mask of doubts,
woven by whispers of fears,
under the cloak of expectations
there is a steady rhythm -
a quiet pulse of light.

You need to peel away the layers,
One by one.

*You are not discovered*
*You are revealed.*

A truth uncovered,
Not created,

*a light that has always been,*
*Waiting to shine.*

# This is How We Begin

Some of us carry stories
etched in the cracks of old walls,
woven through the threads of worn clothes

**tales of struggle, kept in silence.**

We do not hustle to shine in borrowed lights,
nor race in lanes not meant for us.
We strive to rewrite the narrative,
to lift our families beyond the weight of yesterdays,

**to build bridges, if not bridges, at least windows, where
once stood walls.**

Our fight is not to win their battles,
but to conquer the ones they never could.

May we find strength in our quiet persistence,
and courage in every unseen step.

May hope be our compass,
leading us closer to the future
**that once seemed too far to reach.**

# Like The Moon

**A part of you**
isn't there.
There's a void
somewhere
you've been trying to fill
for a long time now.
You try to be happy -
and
you are
not.
You've lost something,
and you don't even know
*what it is.*

Is it
your soul? your mind? your heart?
Or just... your shine?

Don't worry.

Like the moon,
you too
must pass through phases
**to be whole again.**

# Fought With Love

I have seen people
not caring for anything—
*when they are being cared for.*
I have seen people
not thinking of hunger—
*when there is plenty to eat.*
I have seen people
unbothered by crisis—
*when abundance surrounds them.*
I have seen people
not thinking about life—
*while they have one to live.*

Yet, they break down
over the smallest things.

And then -
I have seen **mothers**
sacrificing,
their care,

their food,
their abundance,
and even their life—
to fight a battle
every single day.

A quiet, relentless war
against the odds—
like warriors,
teaching us that even wars
can be won
with just...

**love.**

# The Fire Within

They may not understand
why you light candles in a world
that keeps blowing them out.

Still, you light them.

You might be too gentle
for voices that only know how to shout.

Still, you whisper the truth.

You'll offer love
where others build walls.

Still, your hands stay open.

There will be days
when what you give
feels like it disappears into silence.

Still, you give.

Not because the world asked for it,
but because it's what rises in you
when no one's watching.

It's not about being seen.
It's about staying true—
even when it would be easier not to.

Because the fire inside you
was never lit for applause.

It was lit
so you could see
Yourself.

# You Never Truly Lose

For the longest time in your life, you will fear failure.

What if you aren't good enough?
What if you tried & still lost ?

Initially you will hesitate and then overthink.
You will look around and search for answers and hope
that somebody guides you towards the answers for the
questions in your head.

Stop looking around and work on yourself.

You need to read, learn & grow.

You will stumble, you will get up and you will keep
going.

You will not even realise and the fear of failure will start
fading.

It might not leave but it will lose the power over you.

Because, fear isn't real
when your focus is on growth.

And once you grow,
you never truly lose.

# Quiet Mornings, Loud Minds

Sometimes, you wake up and while brushing your
teeth, you overthink.
Overthink, at the beginning of the day, and you know it
is going to be a long day.
You have thoughts in your head that seem to
appear in the mirror, while everyone else just sees
a reflection.

*You don't need to listen to anyone about anything -*
*just listen to the beat of your own heart.*

Because you need layers of understanding,
and to the world,
you just woke up and are brushing your teeth.

# Firefly

Yes, you've been awake for a while now.
It's noontime -
and still, no one to greet you with a "good morning" text.
You're tired of giving half-hearted answers
to questions that barely scratch the surface.
"How was your day?" *Fine.*
"How's life treating you?" *Beautiful.*

And maybe, just maybe...
you're done.
Done caring for people all the time.
Done watering the plant
and never seeing it bloom.

But

Be kind, even when you're exhausted.
Listen to others, even when no one listens to you.

Say *I love you,*
say *I believe in you,*
even when they don't say it back.

The world is already filled with butterflies.
You, be a firefly.
Because in the darkest hour,
it's not the butterflies
who bring the light.

It's you.

# The Other Turn

All of a sudden,
they'll try to teach you—
what's right,
what's fair,
what you *should* do,
how to behave,
how to smile politely,
all the time, everywhere.
But beyond
the pseudo smiles
and polished etiquette,
there exists a place
risky, raw, and real.

A place where
you might lose people you love,
sacrifice dreams you once cradled.
They'll warn you about this place.
They'll call it dangerous.
They'll steer you toward

the smooth highway of happiness
the safe, easy road.
They'll map it out for you,
build signs,
draw arrows,
wrap it in approval,
and ask you to follow.

But the ones who turned away,
who took the unpaved path
they're the ones who went on road trips
with no maps,
no fixed stops,
learning something new
at every bend.

Because those who follow their heart,
don't live half-lives.
They don't wear masks.
They're not pseudo
they're real.

And there's no one,
absolutely no one,
who can teach you
how to be *you.*

# Cactus

**To the young hearts
who were neglected by their own,**
This is for you.

Growing up for you
must have felt
like the growth of a cactus -
alone, in harsh weather,
with no one in sight.

You learned to raise yourself
when no one stayed to guide you.
You've longed for the love and warmth
you always deserved
but never quite received.
At times,
you might wonder why
you had to walk through
what you did.

And yet, here you are.
You did. You still do.

But here's the thing about the cactus:
It knows how to survive.

*The rainstorms.*
*The burning sun.*
*The long, empty stretches of silence.*
*It thrives through extremes.*

The harshness didn't break you,
It taught you how to endure.

This is for the young hearts
who were neglected by their own -
you're still growing,
and that
is your quiet, unshakable strength.

# Outgrown

Yes, that's how it is.
It seems unfair
but if life *were* fair,
Would you have ever paused to reflect?
Yes, people change.
Feelings shift.
"I miss you" turns into
"At work, text you later."
"Take care" fades into
"I don't care."
And the things that once meant the world
eventually lose their weight.

Remember that sweater you adored as a child?
The one you wore all the time
or those roller skates you couldn't live without?
You never wanted to let them go.

But one day,
you realized you had outgrown them.

So you folded them gently
and tucked them away in a safe corner of your closet.
That's how we do with people too,
don't we?

When the tunnel feels too dark to bear,
and the chaos inside you grows louder,
you find yourself moving
towards the other side,
towards the light,
towards a new beginning.
And what remains behind
is not darkness,
but a closet filled with memories and people
you once fit into

*safe, secure,*
*but no longer meant for where you're going.*

# Kaleidoscope

Maybe you are not in a state to absorb light, and that's
okay.
But that doesn't mean you have to be in the dark all
the time.

*You are a kaleidoscope*

even if you can't absorb the light
You always can reflect the same
to create beautiful colours.

# The Same Glass

I realized something about holding a tumbler.
We're always taught to see the glass as "half full"
or "half empty."
But no one talks about the **weight** of the glass.
The longer you hold it,
the heavier it feels.
Not because it changed
but because *you* did.
Even the lightest things,
when held too long,
can begin to hurt.
So maybe,
The same goes for what we carry in our hearts.
Some things aren't meant to be held forever.
Maybe **letting go** sooner
isn't weakness
but wisdom.

# Art

**You are art.**
And explanations -
they kill art.
Stop explaining
yourself all the time.
Just
**live.**

# Lost Earphones

It's strange
how we only search
for things once they're lost.
Take an old pair of earphones -
we toss them anywhere,
leave them behind without a second thought.
But the moment they're gone,
we feel the silence.
Suddenly, they mattered.
We search.
Sometimes we replace.
Because that's what we do -
with things,
and often,
with people.
Years pass.
And one day, while digging through a drawer,
we find it.
That same forgotten earphone.
And it brings a smile.

Not because it works -
but because it meant something once.

*This time,*
*we keep it safe.*
*Not because it's needed,*
*but because we finally understand.*

# What You Carry

Sometimes,
we hold onto the very things
that cracked us open -
not because we can't let go,
but because we've carried them for so long,
they've grown into the shape of us.
Familiar pain feels safer
than unfamiliar peace.
And so we wear the weight like a second skin,
calling it identity,
calling it strength.
But let's be honest -
you get nothing
from victimizing yourself.

No medals.
No miracles.
Just the same loop,
spinning quietly behind your eyes.
The world isn't waiting

to reward you
for clinging to what broke you.

The real power?
Is in releasing.
Not forgetting,
but loosening your grip

until your hands are free
to hold something better.

# What Spills is You

They say we are made of emotions

*a little love,*
*a little rage,*

some silence we never speak of,
and joy we're too shy to name.

But it's not just what we feel
It's what we fill ourselves with.
Like a cup,
what spills from us
when life shakes us
depends on what we poured in.
So choose carefully.

*Pour in patience,*
*pour in kindness,*
*pour in wonder.*

Let gratitude settle at the bottom,
and hope float at the top.

Because when the world stirs you hard,
you'll want what overflows
to be something beautiful.

# The Door We Avoid

There's a door.
You know the one.
It doesn't creak,
doesn't call
but it waits.
Behind it
live your insecurities,
your doubts,
the shadows you pretend not to see.
You could close your eyes,
and for a moment,
you might forget it's there.
But pretending darkness isn't in the room
won't make it light.
You could run
and yes,
your legs might grow stronger.
But your mind will tire
from carrying what you keep avoiding.
Because what you don't face

never really leaves.
It just grows quieter,
then louder
when you're alone.

*So stop.*

*Turn around.*

*Open the door.*

*Not to suffer,*
*but to heal.*

*Face it*
*so you can finally walk through it.*

*Free.*

# More Was Never Enough

The one who stands by you,
through silence,
through storms,
is the only one who's truly yours.
The rest come and go
like seasons,
like shadows at dusk.
Still, you chased them,
the ones who clapped when you rose
but vanished when you fell.
You called them your people,
while ignoring the one
who sat beside your broken pieces,
quietly, without needing applause.

*Why didn't you see?*
*Why didn't you feel?*

The body you polish,
the image you build
it's all just dust.

Temporary.

The mind plays tricks,
pulling you into a thousand dreams,
but never once
letting you rest.
It feeds on **'more'**

*more love, more praise,*
*more eyes watching.*

But none of it stays.
What stays
is what was always within.
The quiet truth.
The soul that whispers
when the world gets loud.

But you -
you never listened.

# The One Who Always Stayed

You went looking for yourself
in places that never knew your name.
In hands that held you,
only till their own got full.
In eyes that saw you,
but never really looked.

You searched in loud rooms,
hoping noise would drown the silence within.
You wore masks,
not to hide who you are
but to become what they liked.
And still,
you felt empty.

*Not because you lost yourself,*
*but because you were never missing.*

You were always there
in the quiet moments you ignored,
in the breath you rushed past,
in the mirror you avoided.

You -
not the version they clapped for,
not the one they rejected,
not the one you became to survive.

But the you
who stayed
even when everything else left.

That is the truth.
That is home.
That is enough.

# Peace Without Proof

There was a time
I used to explain everything.
Why I was quiet.
Why I left early.
Why I didn't laugh when they expected me to.
I tried
to fill the silence between what I meant
and what they thought I meant.

But you learn,
after enough blank stares,
enough polite nods,
enough people choosing their version of you -
that it's not worth it.
You stop handing out explanations
like bandages
for wounds no one noticed.
You stop peeling back your layers
for people who only ever look at the surface.
And that's not bitterness.

That's peace.

Let them misunderstand.
Let them wonder.
Let them name you things you've never been.

Because if your truth has to be explained
to be respected -
it's already in the wrong hand.

# Watching Time Fade

It's hard to be here
when everything's always going.

*People.*
*Moments.*
*Even feelings,*
*they don't stay long anymore.*

Everyone's moving
somewhere,
anywhere,
as long as it's away
from stillness.

But I've started sitting in it.
The quiet.
The awkward.
The now.

I've started noticing
how the sun touches the wall differently at 4 p.m.,
how tea cools in your hands
before you've even had a sip,
how someone's voice changes
when they're trying not to cry.

And that's the art, isn't it?

Not clinging.
Not chasing.
Just being -
Completely
in a moment
you know won't last.

This world keeps disappearing.
I just choose to stay long enough
to watch it go.

# A Gift

The greatest lesson you will ever learn
is that the world will give you beauty,
but it will also give you pain.
There will be moments
when the weight is too much,
when you question if you can keep going.

But in those moments,
there's something quiet
waiting to be understood:
this, too, is a gift.

The hurt, the struggle,
the emptiness
they are not punishments,
but pieces of the whole.

They shape you,
mold you into something
you wouldn't be without them.

The world will always hand you both.
The joy, the sorrow.
The light, the dark.
And both are necessary.

You won't always understand why,
but you'll learn to accept
that every part of this journey
is meant to be.

*This, too, is a gift.*

# Tinnitus : An Unseen Companion

I was recently diagnosed
with something I can't switch off.

**Tinnitus**

a constant sound
with no beginning,
no end.

It lives inside my head,
but echoes through my days.
A high, invisible thread
woven through moments
that used to be quiet.
At first,
I resisted it
fought it like a storm
I thought would pass.
I lost sleep.

I lost peace.
I lost the kind of silence
I never knew I was lucky to have.

But slowly,
I began to understand:
this sound,
this uninvited guest,
was not going anywhere.

*And isn't that just like life?*

The way pain lingers,
the way thoughts spiral,
the way grief doesn't knock
before it moves in.
The way we carry
what no one else can see.

Tinnitus became more than a sound;
it became a mirror.
Of how we live with the things
we don't choose.
Of how we keep walking
through noise we never asked for.

It taught me

*that not every struggle has to be defeated*
some we learn to live with.
Some we learn to carry
without letting them bury us.

It taught me
*that silence is not the absence of sound*
but the moment
we choose stillness,
even with the noise.

And somehow,
through all of it,
I've grown quieter inside.
Not in defeat,
but in strength.
Not in denial,
but in acceptance.

**This noise may never leave
but neither will I.**

# Even Rocks Break

They say,
"You're strong."
And you smile,
because you're used to it now.

No one sees
how heavy it is
to always be the one

*holding the umbrella*
*when it's storming on everyone else.*

You're the person they call
when they're falling apart
but where do you go
when you're the one
cracking quietly?

You've mastered the art
of keeping it together

in front of people
who'd never notice if you didn't.

Strength isn't lifting others.
It's knowing when you can't anymore,
and still choosing
to be gentle
with everyone else
as well as
with yourself.

# The Chaos & The Quiet

Some days,
you are the mess.
Plates in the sink,
mind like a crowded hallway,
heart carrying too many things at once.

You cancel plans,
leave texts unread,
and sit quietly
with the noise inside your head.

*You fall apart*
*but not loudly.*
*Just enough to feel it.*

And some days,
you are the calm.
The sun rests on your window,
the bed is made,
and you hold space for others

like you weren't unravelling yesterday.

**You are both.**

The storm
and the eye within it.
The silence in the room
and the scream you swallowed last week.
The hand that shakes
and the one that steadies others.
You were never meant
to be only one thing.

You are allowed
to be every version of yourself
and still be home
in your own skin.

# What Age Teaches

When you're younger,
you ask why
like the answer will fix something.

Why they left.
Why it happened.
Why it hurt the way it did.

You think there's closure
waiting at the end of every sentence.
You think one day
you'll find the perfect explanation
that'll make the ache go away.

But growing older
teaches you this:
some things
just don't explain themselves.

Some questions

just stay questions.
And that's okay.

You learn to carry them
without needing to solve them

*like old photos,*
*kept in a box,*
*tucked away*
*but never thrown.*

# Everyday Love

Loving yourself
isn't a shout in the mirror.
It's not a caption,
not a performance,
not a glow-up.

It's the quiet choice
to eat on time.
To stop checking your phone
for people who stopped checking in.
To cry without guilt.
To take a walk
because your mind needs space.

It's not loud.
It's the background music
always playing,
even when no one else hears it.

Loving yourself

is saying,
**"I matter"**
on days when
no one else is saying it to you.


Not Just Saying
Meaning it.

# To the Dogs, He's Home

Every morning,
before the world rushes into noise,
my father steps outside
with quiet hands
and a bag full of trust.

The dogs wait
not just for food,
but for him.
For the one person
who shows up without asking for anything in return.

He doesn't speak much to them,
but they understand
what consistency feels like.
No lectures, no signs
just bowls filled,
tails wagging,
and an unspoken promise
that kindness doesn't need an audience.

I watch him,
day after day,

*teaching me that compassion*
*isn't a performance.*
*It's a rhythm.*
*A ritual.*

A kind of prayer
you do with your hands.

And the dogs
with eyes that speak in silence
and mouths filled with what the world once overlooked
remind me
that love, when it's true,
doesn't arrive with noise.
It arrives with presence.
Soft steps.
Open hands.
The kind that keeps showing up,
even when no one is watching.

# What My Mom Planted in Me

She never asked for much.
Not applause,
not credit,
not even a pause.

She simply gave.
One piece of herself at a time
so we could build a life
with a little more light
than she ever had.

She was the warmth in cold rooms,
the quiet in chaos,
the hand that never let go,
even when we didn't know we were holding it.

She taught us how to be kind
in a world that sometimes forgets how.

To speak the truth
even when silence was easier.

To love
not for show,
but for real.
Without keeping score.
Without waiting for it to come back.

She lived the lessons
we now carry in our bones
That calm is louder than noise.
That giving doesn't make you less -
it makes you more.

And that staying true to who you are
might just be the greatest form of courage.

All the things we are becoming

She was,
long before we had the words.

# What Remains After Us

**Everything fades.**

The days we thought would last forever.
The people we swore would never leave.
Even the versions of ourselves
we once loved, or feared,
or barely understood.

Time moves like a soft thief
not cruel,
just certain.

**But some things don't fade.**

The way you held someone's shaking hand
without asking why.
The words you spoke
when they didn't even know they needed them.
The warmth you offered
without needing credit.

The kindness that felt too small to matter
it mattered most.

Because life isn't about how loud you lived,
or how long it lasted.
It's about how deeply you were felt
in the hearts
you chose to stay soft in.

And when you're gone
it won't be the noise
they remember

*It'll be the calm
you left behind.*

# The Modulus in Me

Give me positive,
I hold it gently.
Let it stay.
Let it shine.
Give me negative,
I don't push it away
I just hold it differently.

Turn it
into something lighter.
Something soft enough
to carry.

I don't reject pain.
I reshape it.
I don't ignore the dark.
I look at it
until it gives me a reason to move.

Because maybe,
that's how I was built
not to choose what comes in,
but to choose
what I become
because of it.

*Call it math.*
*Call it healing.*
*Call it me.*

# The Gardens That Aren't Mine

I've learned
to be happy
watering plants
that don't grow in my yard.

To stop waiting
for everything I give
to return back to me
in perfect shape.

Some things bloom
just because you gave them a little light.
And that's enough.
It's a quiet kind of joy
watching someone else
become more of themselves,
knowing your hands
helped somewhere in the roots.

Not all kindness is loud.
Not all love is personal.
Sometimes,
what you plant
in someone else's world
will be the thing
that keeps you soft
in yours.

And in time,
what you give freely
always finds its way back

*maybe not as flowers,*
*but as peace.*

# Built to Float

The world will always move
sometimes gently,
sometimes like it's trying to knock the wind out of you.

There will be noise,
uninvited voices,
things that happen outside of you
trying to make a home
inside you.

Don't let them.

You are not a container
for everything that crashes around you.

You are a boat
meant to float,
not to sink under waves
that don't belong to you.

And while the waters rise,
keep building what steadies you.
An oar, a sail,
a reason to keep moving.

**You can't stop the sea.**

But you can stop it
from living in your chest.

And some days
that's enough.

To protect the stillness
inside you
while everything else storms.

# You Weren't Meant for Chains

Before you rush forward,
look down.

At the rope.
The quiet one.

The one that doesn't pull,
but still keeps you from moving.
It's not always made of iron.
Sometimes, it's made of memory.
Of old failures
you've kept on replay.
Of words
you never questioned,
but swallowed like truth.
That's not weakness.

That's what they call
**learned helplessness**

when you stop trying,
not because you can't,
but because somewhere,
you started to believe
you weren't allowed to.

But now you know.
And knowing
is a break in the loop.
Put in your effort.

All of it.

Let your sweat
wash off the old story.
Let your breath
remind you of your power.

What happens next
isn't in your hands.
But trying again,
**believing again**
that is.

And remember this
you're not here
to balance on a stool

and wait for applause.

*You are the elephant
of the jungle,
not the circus.*

# Hazy Sunshine

*for my wife*

You weren't the lightning,
not the storm,
not the grand, loud kind of light
that arrives with noise and leaves just as fast.

You were the warmth
that filtered in
on days when everything else felt cold.

Soft.
Subtle.
But always there.

You stayed
in the parts of me
I thought no one would understand—
the moods, the silences,
the quiet battles

I didn't know how to explain.

You didn't fix the dark.
You didn't try to erase it.

You just stayed
and that changed everything.

Some people are sunshine.
But you
you are the kind that arrives
even through clouds,
even when the sky forgets to be blue.

*You are the hazy kind.*

The steady kind.
The kind I would've missed
if I only looked for brightness.

But I saw you.
And now,
I never look away.

—

*For me, she was the hazy sunshine*
*the light that stayed, even when nothing else did.*

*Maybe for you, it's someone too.*
*Or something.*
*A moment, a memory, or a quiet part of yourself still*
*holding on.*

*Look for it.*
*Not everything bright comes loudly.*

*Sometimes, it's the warmth that stays*
*even through the fog.*

—